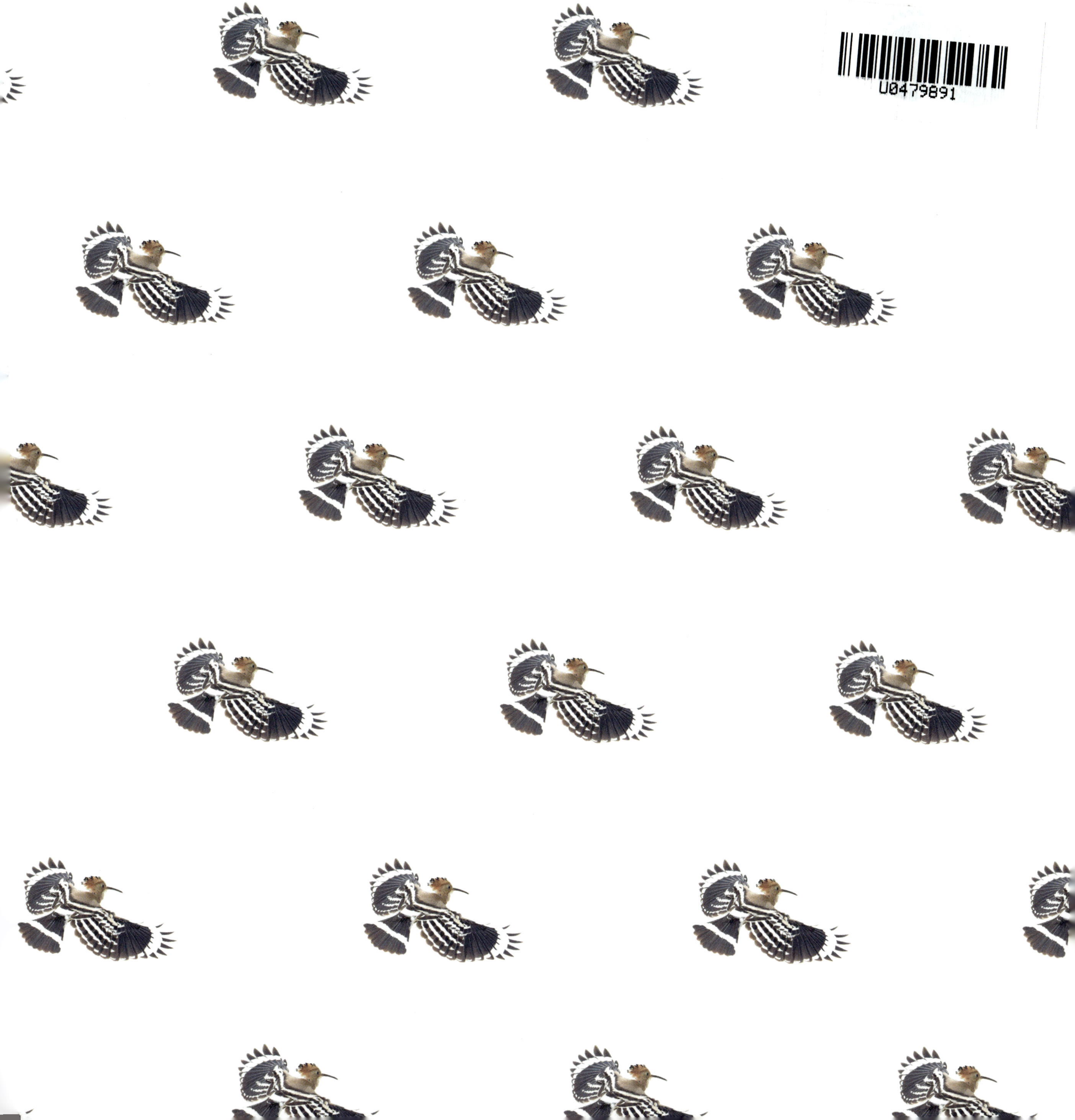

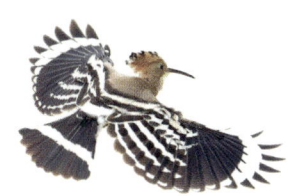

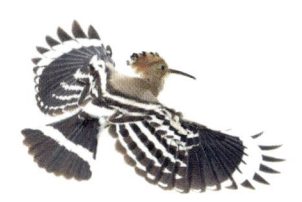

图书在版编目（CIP）数据

鸟类 /（英）哥瑞斯·琼斯著；陈宇彤译 . —西安：世界图书出版西安有限公司，2018.1

（我的动物朋友）

ISBN 978-7-5192-3799-8

Ⅰ. ①鸟… Ⅱ. ①哥… ②陈… Ⅲ. ①鸟类—青少年读物 Ⅳ. ① Q959.7-49

中国版本图书馆 CIP 数据核字（2017）第 276388 号

First published in England in 2017 by Booklife Publishing.
Text and illustrations copyright © 2017 Booklife Publishing.
Bilingual: English-Simplified Chinese translation copyright © 2017 by World Publishing Xi'an Co. Ltd.
Bilingual: English-Simplified Chinese audio, video and APP copyright © 2017 by World Publishing Xi'an Co. Ltd.
All rights reserved.
本书仅限中国大陆地区发行销售。

书　　名	鸟类（我的动物朋友）
著　　者	[英] 哥瑞斯·琼斯
译　　者	陈宇彤
策划编辑	陈宇彤
责任编辑	王　冰
装帧设计	诗风文化
出版发行	世界图书出版西安有限公司
地　　址	西安市北大街 85 号
邮　　编	710003
电　　话	029-87214941　87233647（市场营销部）
	029-87234767（总编室）
网　　址	http://www.wpcxa.com
邮　　箱	xast@wpcxa.com
经　　销	新华书店
印　　刷	鹤山雅图仕印刷有限公司
开　　本	787mm × 1092mm　1/12
印　　张	4
字　　数	20 千字
版　　次	2018 年 1 月第 1 版　2018 年 1 月第 1 次印刷
版权登记	25-2017-0058
国际书号	ISBN 978-7-5192-3799-8
定　　价	45.00 元

版权所有　翻印必究
（如有印装错误，请与出版社联系）

我的动物朋友

鸟 类

[英]哥瑞斯·琼斯/著

陈宇彤/译

动物王国

世界图书出版公司
西安 北京 上海 广州

本书英文原版为英国国家图书馆馆藏图书。本书与英国、美国、加拿大三大英语系国家同步出版。

目录

第 4–5 页

什么是生物?

第 6–7 页

什么是鸟类?

第 8–9 页

它们的栖息地

第 10–11 页

鸟类的家园

第 12–13 页

它们的食性

第 14–15 页

它们如何呼吸?

第 16–17 页

它们如何行动?

第 18–19 页

它们如何生长?

第 20–21 页

光彩夺目的鸟类

第 22–23 页

打破世界纪录的鸟类

什么是生物？

所有的生物都具有生长、发育、繁殖的能力。

生物需要空气、营养、水和阳光。

这些都是生物。

青蛙　　　　老虎　　　　人类

刀，叉，盘子。

书

这些都是非生物。

非生物不具有生长、发育、繁殖的能力。非生物不需要空气、营养、水或阳光，因为它们没有生命气息。

泰迪熊

5

什么是鸟类？

鸟类一般在陆地和水上生存。它们的生存离不开空气、食物、水和阳光。鸵鸟、企鹅和猫头鹰，都属于鸟类。

鸵鸟

资料：

我们已知的鸟类有9000多种。

企鹅

猫头鹰

鸟类拥有双翼，大多擅于飞翔，属脊椎动物。它们是恒温动物，这意味着它们的体温不会随着外界温度的变化而变化。

雪鸮即使在寒冷的环境下依然能够保持温暖，就是因为它们是恒温动物。

它们的栖息地

这种鲜艳亮丽的巨嘴鸟生活在南美洲的热带雨林中。

所有的生物都有它们的**栖息地**或家园。鸟类生活在世界各地的许多不同的栖息地。一些鸟类生活在热带雨林或树林中。

其他鸟类则生活在遍布世界各地的荒漠和山脉中。

这种山地蓝知更鸟生活在北美洲的山脉中。

鸟类的家园

鸟巢

大多数的鸟类，它们生活在特别建筑的家园中，我们称之为鸟巢。鸟巢通常是由泥土、小树枝、树叶和羽毛筑成。鸟类在树上、地面或悬崖岩架上筑巢。鸟巢为它们躲避**捕食者**提供庇护，为它们繁殖、养育雏鸟提供保障。

一些鸟类会迁徙。这意味着它们不会终年生活在同一个地区，而是会飞往不同的地区。当天气变得寒冷时，一些鸟类会飞往**气候**更温暖的地区以躲避严寒。

资料：

每年冬天，燕子会从欧洲飞至非洲。

它们的食性

成年鸟类的食性有食肉、食植物尤其种子等类型，也有杂食类型。一些鸟类会吃其他动物，我们称之为猛禽。猛禽拥有绝佳的视力以帮助它们寻找猎物，同时它们还拥有强壮的脚爪用来捕捉猎物。

金雕

强壮的脚爪

其他一些鸟类是杂食性的。这意味着它们既食肉，也食植物。鸸鹋是杂食性鸟类，它们食用植物（尤其是果实与种子）和昆虫。

鸸鹋

它们如何呼吸?

所有的鸟类都是通过双肺和额外的气囊吸入空气中的氧气来进行呼吸。不同于人类,鸟类的肺在呼气或吸气的过程中不改变大小。

肺

鸟类通过它们喙部顶端的鼻孔呼气和吸气。

鼻孔

它们如何行动？

翅膀

尾巴

肌肉

羽毛

大多数的鸟类擅长使用它们长满羽毛的翅膀在空中飞行。它们动用胸部肌肉来挥动翅膀，借助风来帮助它们在天空中展翅高飞。它们的尾部帮助它们掌控方向。

一只翱翔的信天翁

短而小的翅膀

企鹅

其他鸟类，比如企鹅、鸵鸟，尽管它们拥有翅膀，但却不能飞翔。取代飞翔的是，企鹅学会通过游泳捕捉食物。它们短而小的翅膀帮助它们在水中快速滑行。

它们如何生长？

大部分鸟类在 孵化 前，都是生活在卵里的。有些鸟类，比如黑背信天翁，一次仅能孵化一枚卵，而母鸡却能一次孵化若干枚卵。

待雏鸟孵出后，因为还不会飞翔，这些雏鸟不得不呆在鸟巢中。当它们羽翼丰满并足够强壮时，它们将飞离鸟巢。

资料：
幼鸽大约需要40天才能离开巢穴。

光彩夺目的鸟类

一只雌性孔雀，称作peahen。

一只雄性孔雀，俗称孔雀。

鸟类的羽毛非常亮丽。通常，我们所见的色彩鲜艳的鸟是雄性。因为它们的羽毛越是艳丽，雌性鸟越有可能选择将它们作为自己的**伴侣**。

有些鸟类特别聪明，比如信鸽。人类用信鸽来从一个地区向另一个地区传递信息，这已经有几千年的历史。无论它们飞得有多远，它们仍然能够再次飞回自己的家。

打破世界纪录的
鸟类

鸵鸟

资料：

鸵鸟产下的卵是世界上最大的卵。鸵鸟每小时能跑60公里。

尺寸：
身体高达2.7米

纪录：
世界上最大的鸟类

22

吸蜜蜂鸟

纪录： 世界上最小的鸟类。

尺寸： 身长仅 5厘米

资料： 吸蜜蜂鸟是世界上最小的鸟类，其体重甚至不到几粒米的重量。

23

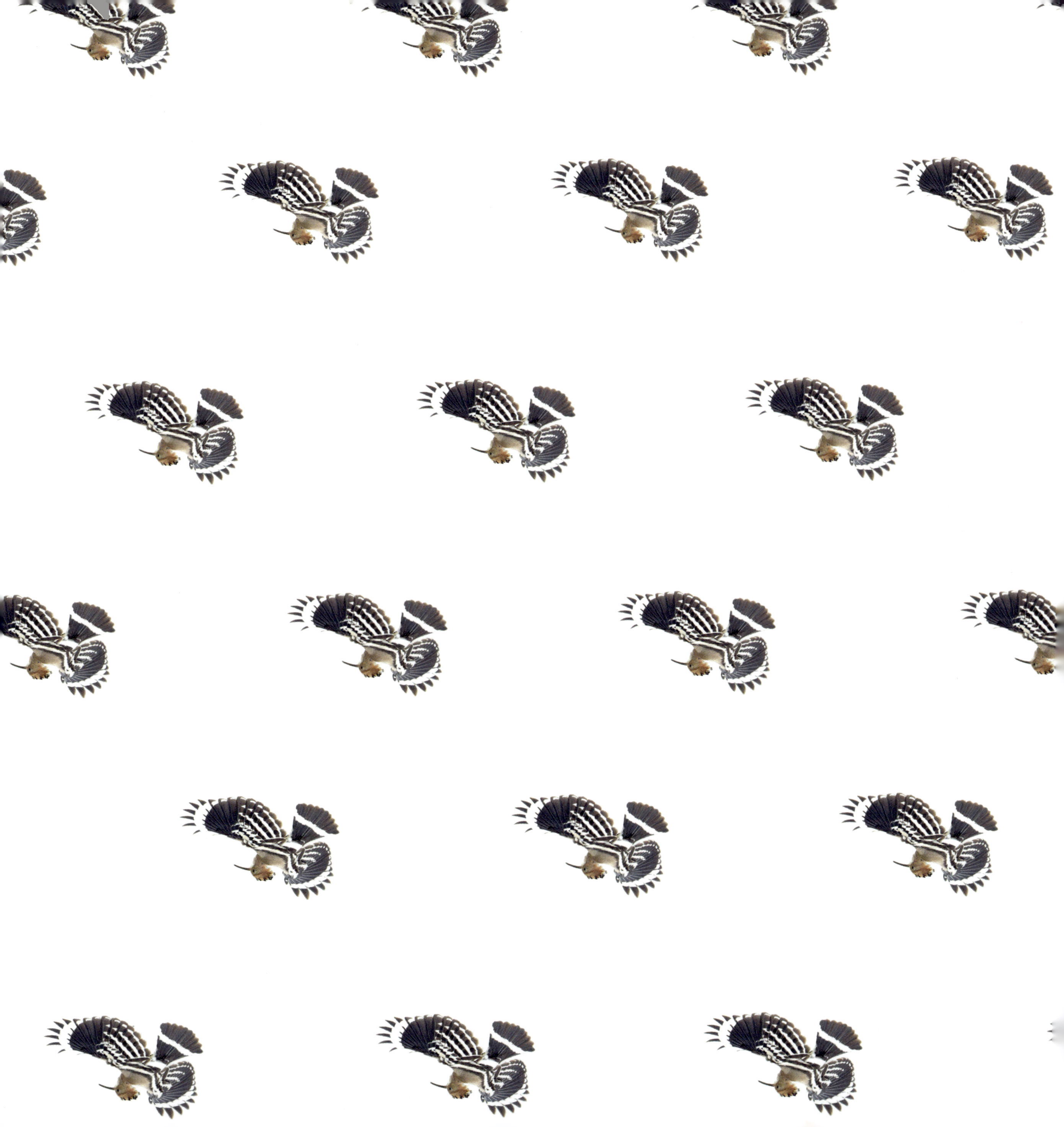

BIRDS

Grace Jones

ANIMAL
KINGDOM

西安 北京 上海 广州

Words that appear like this can be found in the glossary on page 24.

contents

Pages 4-5
What Are Living Things?

Pages 6-7
What Is a Bird?

Pages 8-9
Where Do They Live?

Pages 10-11
Bird Homes

Pages 12-13
What Do They Eat?

Pages 14-15
How Do They Breathe?

Pages 16-17
How Do They Move?

Pages 18-19
How Do They Grow?

Pages 20-21
Brilliant Birds

Pages 22-23
World Record Breakers

Page 24
Glossary & Index

A catalogue record for this book is available from the British Library.

What Are Living Things?

All living things have the ability to grow, develop and reproduce. Living things need air, nutrition, water and sunlight to stay alive.

These are all living things.

Frog

Tiger

Human

Knife, fork & plate.

Books

These are all non-living things.

Non-living things do not have the ability to grow, develop and reproduce. Non-living things do not need air, nutrition, water or sunlight because they are not alive.

Teddy Bear

5

What Is a Bird?

Birds are living things that can live on land and on water. They need air, food, water and sunlight to live. Ostriches, penguins and owls are all types of bird.

Ostrich

Penguin

Owl

Fact: There are over 9,000 known species of birds.

Birds have two wings, can usually fly and have a backbone. They are warm-blooded animals. This means that their body temperature does not change when the temperature does.

A Snowy owl stays warm even when it is freezing cold because it is warm-blooded.

Where Do They Live?

This brightly coloured Toucan lives in the rainforests of South America.

All living things live in a habitat or home. Birds can live in many different habitats around the world. Some birds live in rainforests or woodlands.

Other birds live in the many deserts and mountains that are found throughout the world.

This Mountain Bluebird lives in the mountains of North America.

Bird Homes

A bird's nest.

Most birds live in specially built homes, called nests. They are usually made out of mud, twigs, leaves and feathers. They build their nests in trees, on the ground or in rocky ledges. Nests provide them with shelter from **predators** and a home to breed and raise their babies in.

Other birds migrate. This means that they do not stay in one home, but fly to different ones throughout the year. When the weather becomes colder, some birds will migrate to the hotter climates to stay warm.

Fact: Swallows migrate from Europe to Africa every winter.

What Do They Eat?

Adult birds eat meat or plants, especially their seeds, or a mixture of both. Some birds that eat other animals are called birds of prey. They have very good eyesight to find their food and strong feet to catch and hold onto their prey with.

A Golden Eagle.

Strong Feet

Other birds are omnivorous. This means that they eat both animals and plants. Emus are omnivorous birds; they eat plants, especially their fruits and seeds, and insects.

Emu

How Do They Breathe?

All birds breathe in oxygen from the air through their two lungs and extra air pouches. Unlike humans, birds' lungs do not change size when they breathe in or out.

Lungs

14

Birds breathe in and out through nares that found at the top of their beaks. Their nostrils are called nares.

Nares

15

How Do They Move?

Wings

Tail

Muscles

Feathers

Most birds can fly through the air using their feathered wings. They use breast muscles to move their wings and the wind to help them fly high into the sky. They use their tails to change direction.

A Waved Albatross in flight.

Small, short wings.

Penguin

Other birds, like penguins and ostriches, cannot fly even though they have wings. Instead of flying, penguins have learnt to swim to catch their food. Their small, short wings help them to travel through the water quicker.

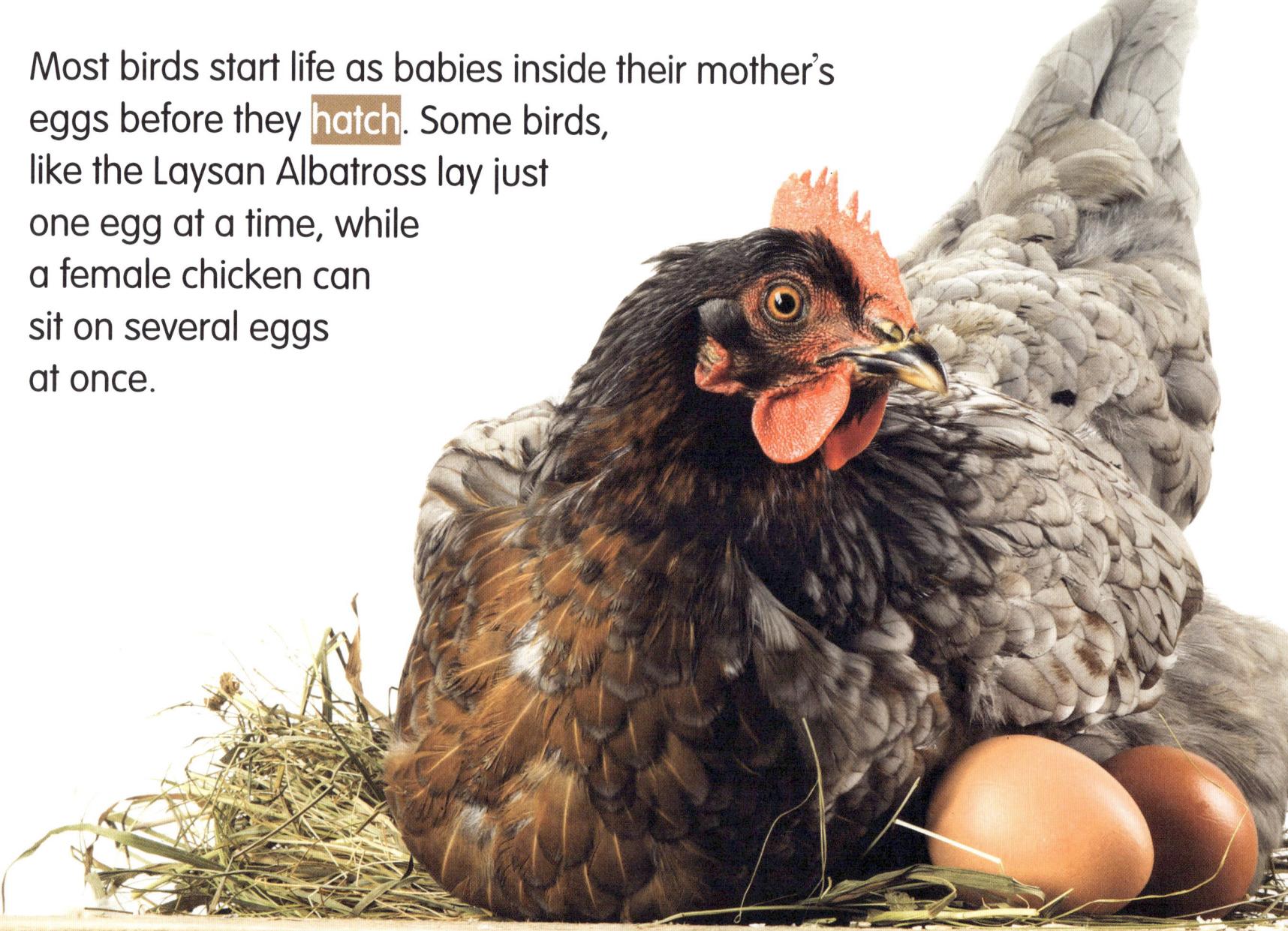

How Do They Grow?

Most birds start life as babies inside their mother's eggs before they hatch. Some birds, like the Laysan Albatross lay just one egg at a time, while a female chicken can sit on several eggs at once.

Once they hatch, the baby birds have to stay in the nest because they cannot fly yet. When their wings have grown bigger and they are strong enough, they fly away from the nest.

Fact: Baby pigeons take around **forty days** to leave the nest.

Brilliant Birds

A female Peafowl, called a peahen

A male Peafowl, called a peacock.

Birds' feathers can be very brightly coloured. Usually, the colourful birds we see are males. This is because the more colourful they are, the more likely it is female birds will choose them as their mate.

Some birds, like homing pigeons, are particularly smart. They have been used for thousands of years to carry messages from country to country. However far they have to travel, they can always find their way home again.

World Record Breakers

OSTRICH

Fact: The ostrich lays the **largest eggs** and can run as fast as **60 kilometres per hour.**

Size: Up to 2.7 metres tall

Record: The World's Biggest Bird

22

BEE HUMMINGBIRD

Record: The World's Smallest Bird

Size: Up to 5 cm long

Fact: The smallest bird in the world **weighs less** than a few grains of **rice!**

23

Glossary

Climates: types of weather in particular places.

Habitat: a home where animals and plants live.

Hatch: when a baby animal or insect comes out of its egg.

Mate: a partner who they choose to have their young with.

Predators: any animal that eats other animals and insects.

Prey: any animal or insect that is eaten by another.

Index

Baby 10, 18, 19
Breathe 14, 15
Eggs 18, 22
Fly 7, 11, 16, 17, 19
Food 6, 12, 17
Grow 4, 5
Homes 8, 10, 11, 21
Living Things 4, 5, 6, 8
Move 16
Nest 10, 19
Wings 7, 16, 17, 19

Photo Credits

Photocredits: Abbreviations: l–left, r–right, b–bottom, t–top, c–centre, m–middle. All images are courtesy of Shutterstock.com.

Front Cover – Mark Bridger. 1 –Eric Isselee. 2–3 – pzAxe. 4bl – Chros. 4c – Eric Isselee. 4r – michaeljung. 5bl – Elena Schweitzer. 5tl – koosen. 5r – Lichtmeister. 6bl – Kotomiti Okuma. 6bc – Phant. 6r – Aaron Amat. 7 – Stanislav Duben. 8 – Oleksiy Mark. 9 – Tom Reichner. 10 – PCHT. 11 – non15. 12tr – withGod. 12b – 秋枫. 13 – Robyn Mackenzie. 13inset – Gunnar Rathbun. 14 – Butterfly Hunter. 14illustration –BlueRingMedia. 15 – Dmitri Gomon. 16 – Neil Burton. 17 – Christian Musat. 18 – Tim UR. 19 – Vishnevskiy Vasily. 20 – Drop of Light. 20inset – kajornyot. 21 – guentermanaus. 22 – Coffeemill. 23tr – 秋枫. 23bl – Andrii Gorulko. 24 – 秋枫. 25 – 秋枫.

ANIMAL KINGDOM

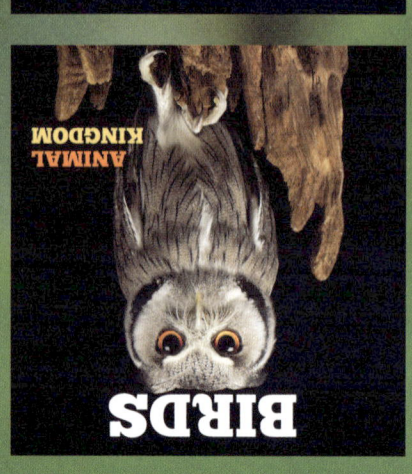

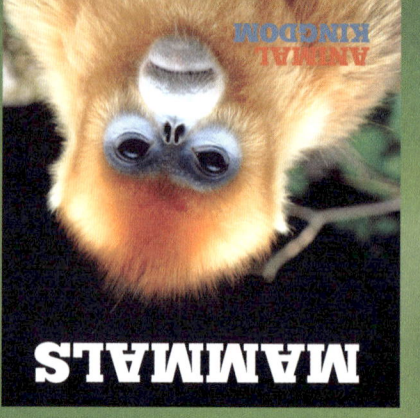

What is a living thing? Where do animals live? What do animals eat? How do they move and grow? Learn the answers to these questions in this exciting new series. With easy to read text and informative diagrams, this series offers a simple introduction to the animals that live in our world.

FISH

REPTILES

AMPHIBIANS

BIRDS

MAMMALS

INSECTS

ANIMAL KINGDOM